ISSUES OF OUR TIME

ALCOHOL ABUSE

Is This Danger on the Rise?

Richard Steins

Twenty-First Century Books

A Division of Henry Holt and Company
New York

Twenty-First Century Books
A division of Henry Holt and Company, Inc.
115 West 18th Street
New York, New York 10011

Henry Holt® and colophon are registered trademarks of Henry Holt and
Company, Inc.
Publishers since 1866

Published in Canada by Fitzhenry & Whiteside Ltd.
195 Allstate Parkway, Markham, Ontario L3R 4T8

Printed in the United States of America
Series Editor: Tanya Lee Stone

Created and produced in association with Blackbirch Graphics, Inc.

Library of Congress Cataloging-in-Publication Data

Steins, Richard.
    Alcohol abuse: is this danger on the rise? / Richard Steins. — 1st ed.
        p.   cm. — (Issues of our time)
    Includes index.
    ISBN 0-8050-3882-5 (acid-free paper)
    1. Alcoholism—United States—Juvenile works. 2. Alcoholics—United States—
Family relationships—Juvenile literature. 3. Alcoholics—Rehabilitation—United
States—Juvenile literature. 4. Alcoholism—Treatment—United States—Juvenile
literature. I. Title. II. Series.
HV5072.S915   1995
362.29'2'0973—dc20   95-19445
                                                                        CIP
                                                                        AC

Contents

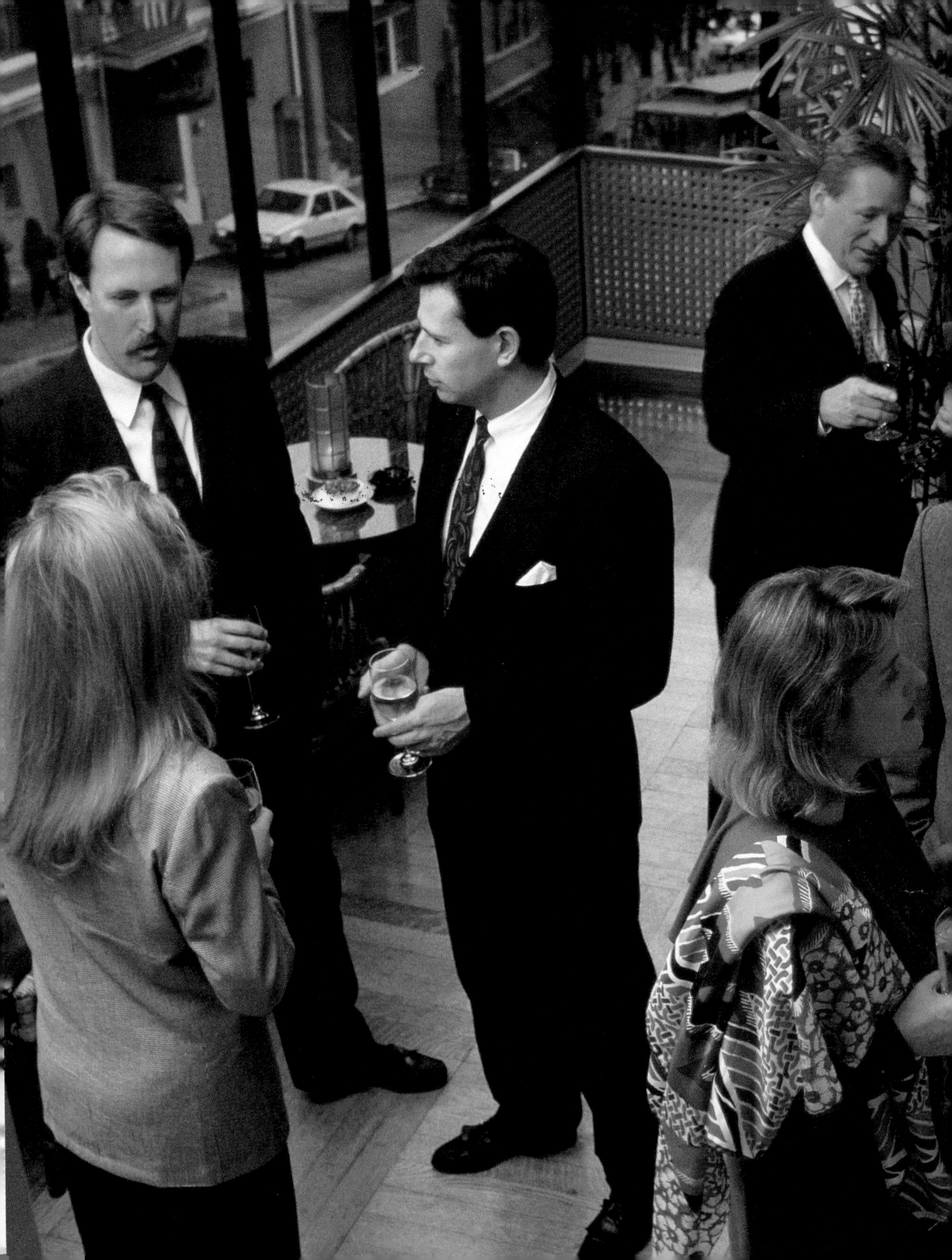

1

......

Alcohol Abuse: Human Weakness or Disease?

Lincoln School Library

Millions of Americans drink alcoholic beverages—beer, wine, wine coolers, or hard liquors, such as scotch, gin, and vodka. Many adults love to sit in front of the television watching football or other sports and sipping beer. Others will have a glass or two of wine with dinner. We often celebrate birthdays and weddings with a toast. Sometimes, when a person has a hard day on the job, he or she may like to "unwind" with a drink before dinner. More than 70 percent of adult Americans drink alcohol in some form. About 10 percent of those who drink alcohol abuse it.

Most of us are probably familiar with what happens when a person has had too much to

Social drinking among adults occurs most often at celebrations and other gatherings. Unlike alcoholics, however, people who have an occasional drink are not addicted to alcohol.

An alcoholic sleeps on a busy New York City street. Alcoholics who do not confront their disease can lose control of their lives and eventually die.

drink. Some people can have a number of drinks and not seem to change, but others can have only one drink and are affected by it. People who have had too much to drink usually undergo behavioral changes. They may slur their words and become loud. Some become happy, while others become very sad. A few people may even become violent. A person who has had too much to drink may stagger, fall down, or pass out. Or, a person may suffer something even more severe called a blackout. During a blackout, a person does and says things he or she cannot later remember. People who abuse alcohol get drunk, and after having too much to drink, many people will wake up with a hangover—headache, nausea, and generally ill feelings the morning after.

Alcohol—whether it is in wine, beer, or hard liquor—is a drug. It travels immediately into the bloodstream and to the brain, where it affects our central nervous system. Even a small amount of alcohol will depress the central nervous system. After first making a person feel "high," the alcohol is likely to leave the drinker feeling down, or depressed.

Is alcohol abuse a human weakness? Many people believe it is. They argue that those who drink too much are weak and lack self-control. But in the last fifty years, we have acquired new understandings about excessive drinking. We now know that alcohol abuse may be a sign of a disease known as alcoholism. And people who suffer from this disease are known as alcoholics.

What Is Alcoholism?

Alcoholism is a disease in which a person is unable to stop drinking even though it is causing that person harm. An alcoholic has a compulsion—an uncontrollable urge—to drink despite the damaging consequences. A person who is not an alcoholic is able to simply stop drinking—or not drink at all—whenever he or she chooses. A

A normal liver (left) is pictured next to a liver that is fatty from alcohol disease (middle) and a cirrhotic liver (right) that was destroyed by cirrhosis.

nonalcoholic does not *need* to drink. An alcoholic, however, *cannot stop* drinking once he or she has had the first drink.

Alcoholism is also a progressive disease—the alcoholic's condition gets worse as he or she continues to drink. The end result of severe alcoholism is death. Alcoholism affects people physically and psychologically in a number of ways. It can lead to:

• the destruction of brain cells, causing loss of memory and a decreasing ability to learn;

• cirrhosis of the liver, a condition in which the liver hardens, develops scar tissue, and eventually stops functioning;

• diseases of the digestive system;

• diseases of the heart; and

• psychological and emotional disorders, including changes in personality, depression, and even suicide.

How Can We Tell If
Someone Is an Alcoholic?

The National Institute on Drugs and Alcohol (NIDAA) has published a checklist that can be used to help determine if someone has an alcohol abuse problem. Here are a few of the yes/no questions on their list.

Does the person:

- drink frequently to escape from stress or problems?
- drink more than most people?
- drink alone?
- feel guilty about drinking and promise to drink less?
- blame others for his or her drinking problem?
- deny there is a drinking problem?
- sometimes forget what happened during a drinking period?
- lose time from work or school because of drinking?
- lose control when drinking?
- have physical complaints that may be related to drinking?

A "yes" to one or more of these questions may be a sign that a person has a problem with alcohol abuse.

Alcoholism in
the United States

Alcoholism is one of the most devastating diseases in our country. Some five million Americans are believed to be alcoholics. But they are not the only ones who suffer. Their

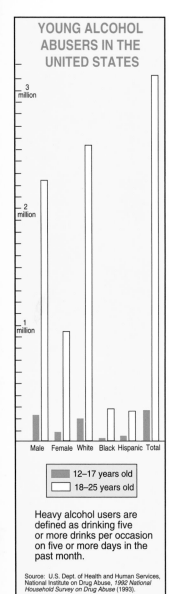

YOUNG ALCOHOL ABUSERS IN THE UNITED STATES

3 million

2 million

1 million

Male Female White Black Hispanic Total

■ 12–17 years old
□ 18–25 years old

Heavy alcohol users are defined as drinking five or more drinks per occasion on five or more days in the past month.

Source: U.S. Dept. of Health and Human Services, National Institute on Drug Abuse, *1992 National Household Survey on Drug Abuse* (1993).

immediate families, friends, and even the American economy feel the impact, too. Alcoholism results in the loss of approximately $45 billion a year in terms of lost jobs and income, hospital costs, and illnesses, deaths, and accidents related to excessive drinking.

Who becomes an alcoholic? Even though we know more today about alcoholism than we did in the past, we are still not completely certain why some drinkers become alcoholics and others do not. We know, for example, that alcoholism tends to run in families. A person whose parents or grandparents were alcoholics has a much greater chance of becoming an alcoholic than someone from a family with no history of the disease.

We also know that certain groups of people are more likely to suffer from alcoholism, although we are not certain why this is so. For example, people from countries in northern Europe have a higher rate of alcoholism than people who live in southern Europe. But many people in both these regions drink alcohol regularly. Why does one group have a higher rate of alcoholism than the other?

Professionals who treat alcoholism describe it as a complicated disease. Some people believe that alcoholics have inherited a gene that makes them more likely to get the disease. Others think alcohol abuse is a learned behavior. That is, people who grow up surrounded by family and friends who

Alcoholism and Denial

When you develop a sore throat and runny nose, you probably say to yourself, "I'm getting a cold." Most people suffering from alcoholism, however, will deny that they have an illness. In fact, denial is one of the main symptoms of alcoholism.

Why is this so? Why do people suffering from a serious illness deny that they have it and prevent themselves from getting treatment? Part of the answer is that most people still do not understand that alcoholism is a disease. The alcoholic continues to believe that he or she can stop drinking at any time. Diseases, however, do not work that way. If you have a serious illness, you must see your doctor and take medication to get better. Otherwise, your condition will only get worse. The same is true for the alcoholic.

Society also plays a role in alleviating some of the seriousness of this problem. Drinking is often associated with many positive feelings. At first, a drink may make a person feel relaxed and in good spirits. We tend to forget what happens once someone has too much to drink. Drinking is also a part of many happy events in our lives: parties, special dinners, or watching sports on television with friends, which makes it seem acceptable.

Since drinking is a normal part of many people's lives, the significance of *excessive* drinking is sometimes overlooked. On occasion, we may even laugh at drunken behavior. The good-natured drunk who says silly things and falls down is a familiar, supposedly amusing character in movies. While we would feel sorry for someone who has cancer, we still find drunkenness to be funny.

Alcoholics are often aided in avoiding facing their illness by well-meaning friends and family members who downplay their problem. For example, if Dad is home with a hangover, Mom may call work for him and say that he cannot go in because he has a cold. Because family members often do not want to face the consequences of confronting the problem, they will help cover it up. In doing so, they assist the alcoholic in denying the seriousness of the problem.

Finally, the alcoholic is usually reluctant or afraid to admit that he or she may have a problem. Alcoholics who face their disease usually do so only when they have reached a point of severe crisis, such as a lost job, a divorce, or a serious illness. Only when the protective armor of denial is cracked can the alcoholic hope to begin recovery.

drink too much may learn this behavior. It may also be some combination of these factors. Alcoholism today is considered a disease and not merely a human weakness. Nevertheless, an alcoholic can get better only if he or she acts responsibly and admits that there is a problem.

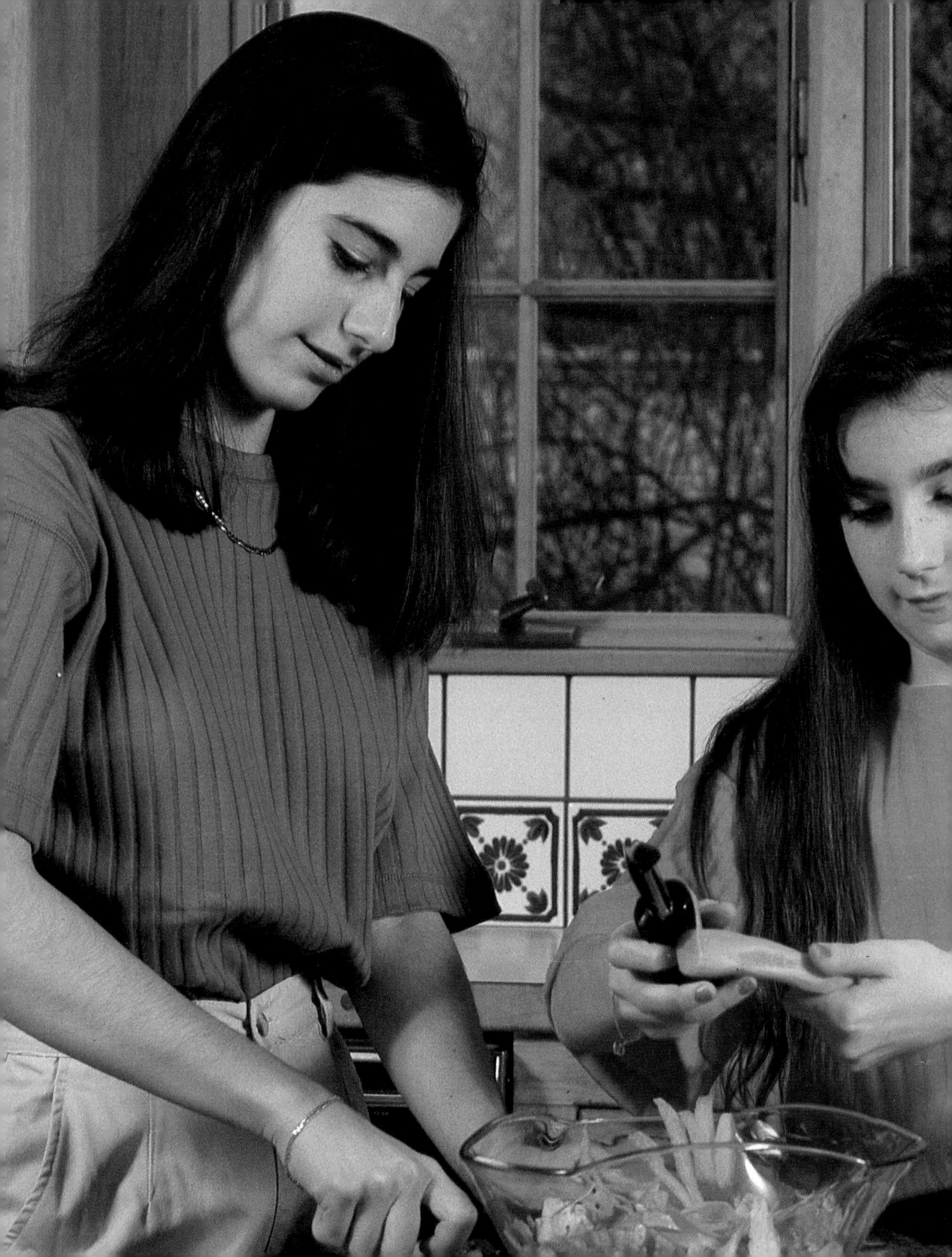

2
....

Alcohol Abuse and the Family

Alcoholism is often called a family disease. A 1987 hearing before Congress revealed that 28 million Americans—or about 12 percent of the population—grew up in families where one or both parents were alcoholics. Today, that number is estimated at about 35 million. But the alcoholic is not the only one affected by the disease. In a family where one or both parents abuse alcohol, every member of the family is touched by that abuse in some way.

Much of what we learn as children comes from our family. Our parents serve as role

Alcoholic parents often neglect their children's needs. As a result, children of alcoholics often have to assume their parents' responsibilities.

models and teach us right from wrong. They also provide us with food, clothing, and shelter while we are growing up. Our values, religious beliefs, and habits are all shaped by our family from the time we are infants. A stable family produces healthy children who have high self-esteem—that is, children who feel good about who they are. When children from these families become adults, they often have their own families and get the chance to be strong, fit parents.

Life With Alcohol Abusers

In an alcoholic family, life is turned upside down. Alcoholic parents make poor role models. When they are drinking, they cannot be there to teach their children values because they are too busy being drunk or suffering from hangovers. Also, alcoholic parents are often frightening to be around. Their drinking usually leads to behavior changes and maybe even to violence. A child in an alcoholic family never knows what to expect from the parents. Even in families where a parent's drinking is not advanced, the children still suffer. Children of alcoholics (COAs) always talk about never being able to count on their alcoholic parent.

One of the most damaging results of poor parenting is that children often blame themselves for a parent's drinking. They think, "If I wasn't

Ignored Alcoholism: Alcohol Abuse Among the Elderly

In general, people tend to drink less as they get older. Still, the U.S. government estimates that about 10 percent of people over the age of sixty abuse alcohol. Some of the pressures of old age—illness, the death of friends and family, boredom, perhaps even reduced income—may explain why the elderly turn to alcohol.

Alcohol can have extremely damaging effects on older people. Because the liver processes the alcohol more slowly in elderly people, the alcohol remains in the system longer. As a result, it can cause more damage, especially to the brain. For example, older people often suffer memory loss as they age, and alcohol can further aggravate this problem. Elderly people who abuse alcohol may forget to eat and take medications, and may be more prone to accidents.

The effects of alcohol are also often made worse in older people because they frequently take medications for other ailments. The combination of alcohol and some medications can be deadly. At the very least, the alcohol may cause the prescription drugs to lose their effectiveness. In addition, the alcohol alone can lead to serious depression among the elderly.

Alcohol abuse among the elderly has often been misdiagnosed or even ignored. In the past, some physicians have tended not to take the elderly quite as seriously as they did their younger patients. Often, an elderly patient with numerous physical complaints may experience difficulty explaining what is wrong to a doctor. Due to this problem, elderly people have sometimes been overmedicated. For complaints of sleep disorders, some doctors in the past have suggested that their patients drink a shot of brandy before going to bed at night.

Today, however, doctors have become more aware of the needs of this segment of the population. There are physicians who specialize in geriatric medicine, which is health care for the elderly. We also have an increased knowledge of how alcohol and medicines interact. Doctors tend to be much more on the lookout for hidden alcohol abuse among the elderly.

bad, Mom wouldn't drink." Children of alcoholic parents grow up with low self-esteem, feeling that they are worthless and may have caused their parents' drinking problems. In this sense, alcoholism is truly a family disease because its bad effects are passed from one generation to another.

Is There an Alcoholic Gene?

Alcoholism is a complex disease and its cause is not completely understood. It may result from a combination of factors. In recent years, scientists have focused on the role that inherited chemical defects may play, especially in families with a history of alcoholism.

In 1990, scientists discovered a rare gene that may increase a person's chances of becoming an alcoholic. This gene, called the dopamine-receptor gene, is believed to be associated with severe alcoholism. Although it appears that only a small percentage of alcoholics have this gene, it may explain the origin of some forms of alcoholism in those individuals.

Scientists have stressed that there are still millions of alcoholics who do not carry this gene. Their disease must be a result of other factors, as yet undetermined. Because of this discovery, however, we now know that the tendency to become an alcoholic may be part of our physical makeup—something inherited from our parents, like the risk of heart disease or diabetes.

COAs also may not have their basic needs met. When parents are drunk, there is no one to cook meals, do laundry, or shop for groceries. A parent may even lose a job due to drinking.

Families suffer terribly from alcoholism. The divorce rate in alcoholic families is four times the national average. Suicide rates are higher, too—60 percent of all teenagers who attempt suicide come from alcoholic families. Incidents of violence, child abuse, sexual abuse, and incest are also higher in alcoholic families than in healthy families.

Warning Signs of an Alcoholic Family

Just because your parents drink alcohol does not mean that you live in an alcoholic family. But there are a number of warning signs that a family may have a problem with alcohol.

• Do either of your parents drink to the point that their behavior changes? Do they argue, get abusive or violent, or neglect their responsibilities?

• Does your parents' drinking affect you in some way? Do you have trouble doing your schoolwork? Are you afraid when your parents drink?

• Do you feel that you are responsible for your parents' drinking? Do you feel you need to do something to make them stop drinking?

• Do you avoid admitting to yourself or anyone else that there may be an alcohol abuse problem in your home?

• Do you avoid bringing friends home because you don't know how your parents will behave if they've been drinking?

• Do you sometimes feel your whole family is crazy and that something is wrong with you, too?

If you answer "yes" to one or more of these questions, your family may be suffering from a problem with alcohol abuse.

COAs and
ACOAs Professionals who treat families affected by alcoholism refer to the children who live in these families as COAs. COAs have many things in common as a result of their similar family experiences. They tend to have low self-esteem and feel depressed a lot of the time. They often feel guilty

A teenager participates in a counseling session. When one member of a family suffers from alcoholism, the entire family is affected.

and lonely and are afraid that their families will break up. They also have trouble trusting people, mainly because their parents have kept very few, if any, of their promises. Family life centers on the alcoholic and his or her behavior. Since all the attention is focused on someone else, COAs usually grow up believing that no one loves or cares about them.

COAs are at much greater risk of becoming alcoholics than children from nonalcoholic families. They are five times more likely to become problem drinkers themselves. Why would a child who has been exposed to all the terrible effects of excessive drinking have a greater chance of becoming an alcoholic? Shouldn't the opposite be true?

One possible explanation is that alcohol offers a temporary escape from problems. After taking a drink, a COA may feel relaxed and powerful and able to handle the problems of living in a troubled family. COAs never get the opportunity to develop the emotional and social skills necessary to resolve conflict and to develop as healthy adults. Deprived of these experiences, these children often turn for relief to the very drug that has been the source of their misery in the first place—alcohol.

Adults who have grown up in alcoholic families are referred to by professionals as ACOAs (adult children of alcoholics). ACOAs carry the experiences and suffering of their childhood into maturity. Like COAs, they usually have low self-esteem and are depressed. Because watching how their alcoholic parents acted toward each other provided a poor role model for them, ACOAs frequently have difficulty forming relationships. And like COAs, they have a greater risk of becoming alcoholics themselves or of marrying an alcoholic.

In order to recover from damaging childhoods, ACOAs must learn to experience and express the anger and sense of betrayal that they feel. And they must grieve for their lost childhood. Kids growing up in alcoholic families learn not to get angry, out of fear of upsetting the alcoholic parent. Anger, a normal human emotion, is something that ACOAs dread. But years of holding anger back causes serious damage. ACOAs often turn to drink themselves to deaden their anger and pain.

Many also develop eating disorders, such as anorexia and bulimia. Anorexia is a disease that affects mostly young women. Anorexics often

starve themselves to death, believing that they are fat and must control their weight by not eating—even when they weigh as little as 80 pounds. Bulimics will eat huge amounts of food in one sitting and then force themselves to vomit or use laxatives. Bulimia is sometimes called the "binge and purge" disease. Eating disorders such as anorexia and bulimia are complex diseases that are difficult to cure. Most professionals believe they are the result of low self-esteem and are attempts to exert control in the lives of people who feel depressed and out of control. Both diseases are also considered slow forms of suicide, of anger turned in on itself.

What Is
Co-dependence?

Co-dependence is a concept that developed in the 1960s and 1970s among professionals treating people who were dependent on alcohol and drugs. These professionals noted that the loved ones of those being treated shared similar problems. They gradually came to realize that the husbands, wives, and loved ones of alcoholics had a disease themselves—co-dependence.

In its simplest terms, co-dependence is an unhealthy way of living, thinking, and coping that results from living with an alcoholic. A person who is co-dependent orients his or her life around the alcoholic's life. In co-dependent families, feelings are often not discussed. In the words of a recovering alcoholic, "The alcoholic is wrapped around the bottle, and the co-dependent is wrapped around the alcoholic."

Co-dependency is another way of describing the condition of being a COA or an ACOA. Some professionals, however, believe that co-dependence applies to many situations, not just to alcoholism, and that it is an addiction in itself. In other words, even though the co-dependent people are suffering, they are addicted to the way they live, in spite of the pain. In order to recover, co-dependents must discover and release their feelings, especially anger. They must also learn to focus on their own needs and not those of the alcoholic.

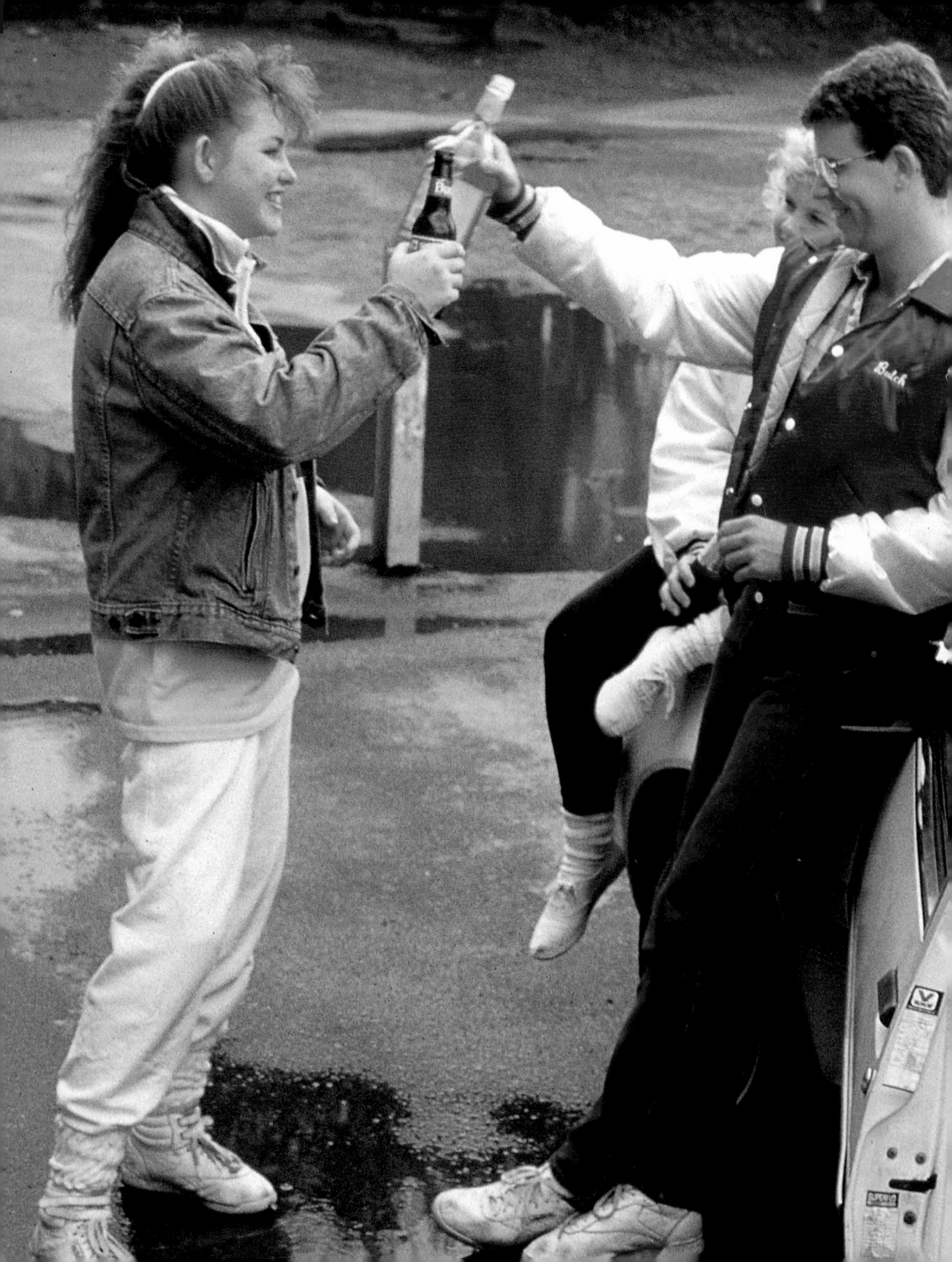
Butch

3
·······

Growing Up
and Drinking

We have learned what alcoholism is and how it affects the family. But what about you as an individual? When you leave your home to go to school or to meet your friends, do your friends pressure you to drink? Do you know anyone in your class who drinks? How serious are the effects of alcohol on young people?

Young People and Alcohol
A government statistic in 1994 showed that more than 10 million of the 21 million children in grades 7 to 12 have tried alcoholic beverages. More than 8 million have a drink at least once a week, and about 500,000 have at least five or more drinks at one time.

Teenagers drink in a public parking lot in New Jersey. Statistics show that people are experimenting with alcohol at younger ages than they have in the past.

CAMPUS DRUNKENNESS		
	Non-binge drinkers	Frequent binge drinkers
Had a hangover	30%	90%
Did something regrettable	14%	63%
Missed a class	8%	61%
Engaged in unplanned sex	8%	41%
Was injured	2%	23%
Damaged property	2%	22%
Got into trouble with police	1%	11%

A binge was defined as having five drinks in a row for a male and four drinks in a row for a female. Frequent bingers had three binges in a two-week period.

Source: *U.S. News and World Report; Journal of the American Medical Association.*

In addition, the age at which kids drink has been going down during this century. In the 1930s, for example, the average boy did not have his first drink until he was seventeen. Girls at that time usually did not try alcohol until they were nineteen. Today, the average age for both boys and girls is twelve, and in some cases children as young as ten are already drinking.

Studies prove that the younger a person is when he or she tries alcohol, the more likely it is that the person will become an adult alcoholic. Another alarming statistic released in 1994 showed that some 80 percent of college students "binge" when they drink—that is, they have more than five drinks in a row and become very drunk. Binge drinking has become a major problem on college campuses, where it is connected with destructive behavior, date rape, violence, and the disruption of college life for those students who choose not to drink.

Heavy drinking on college campuses has also been associated with hazing—the practice of initiating new members into a fraternity by requiring that they do some outrageous stunt, such as drinking a bottle of liquor all at once. Newspapers in recent years have reported more than one case of a young person dying of acute alcohol poisoning during hazing. As a result, most college campuses have now banned extreme forms of hazing.

Columbia University fraternity members take turns drinking large amounts of beer through a funnel. Heavy drinking on college campuses can disrupt life even for non-drinking students.

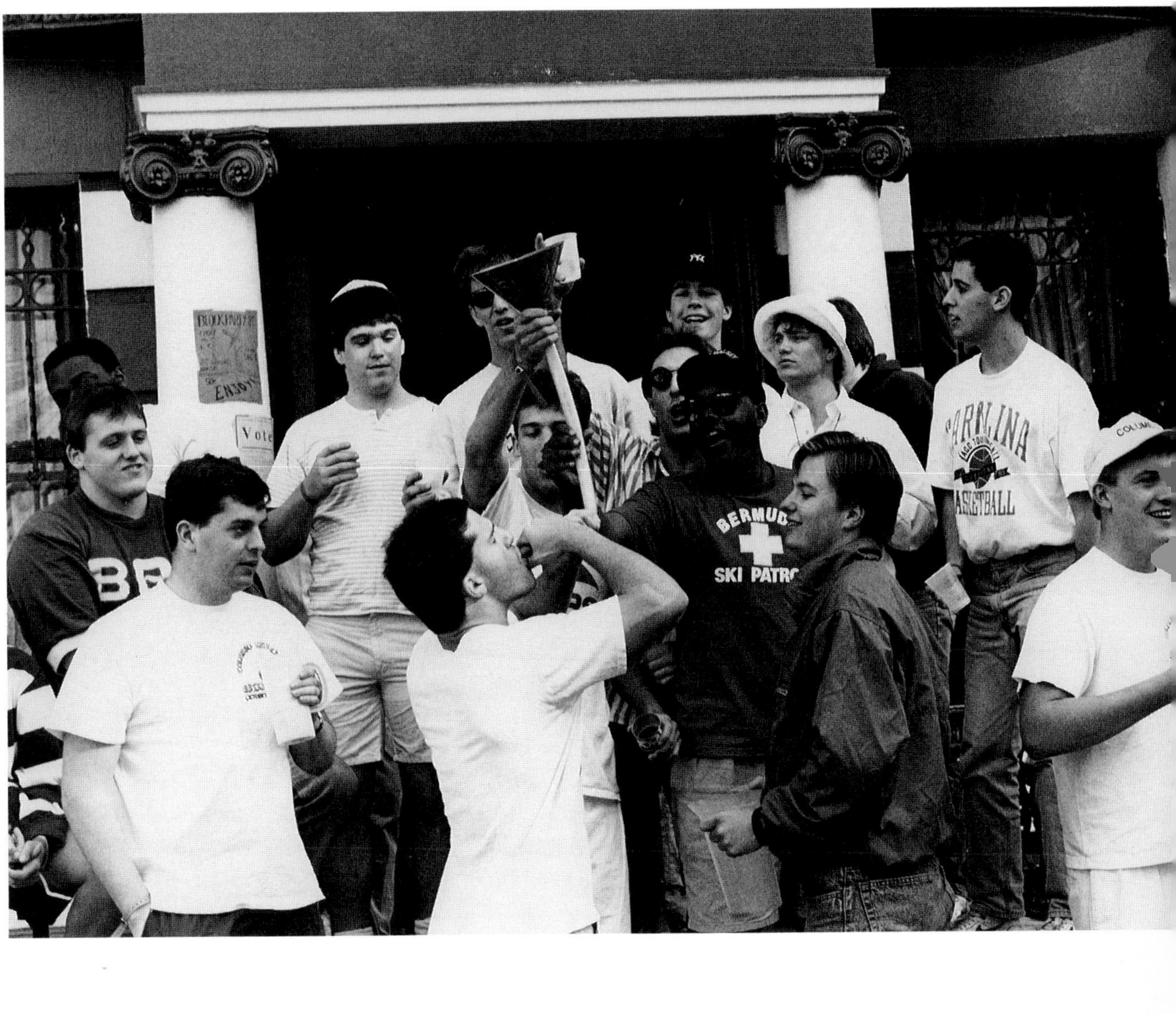
BERMUDA
SKI PATR
BASKETBALL

**Peer Pressure
and Health Issues** How do we explain the fact that young people are drinking—and so destructively as well? Part of the answer is peer pressure. Young people consider drinking as a sign of being grown up, especially if they see their parents doing it. If your friends drink, they may pressure you to join them. Children are especially vulnerable to this because they understandably want to be accepted by their friends and feel like part of the group.

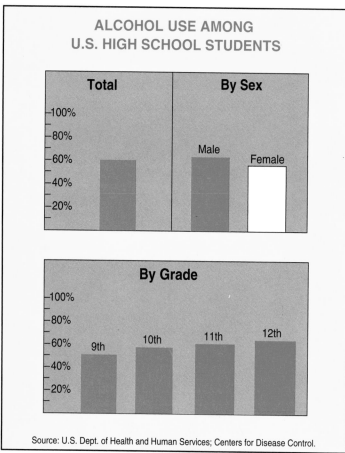

ALCOHOL USE AMONG
U.S. HIGH SCHOOL STUDENTS

Source: U.S. Dept. of Health and Human Services; Centers for Disease Control.

Unfortunately, most young people do not have much knowledge about alcohol and its effects. In fact, a 1991 government study showed that 20 million students did not under-stand why alcohol affects the human body the way it does. Most kids do not know the alcohol content of various drinks. A wine cooler, for example, tastes sweet and may be easy to obtain, even for a minor. Many kids believe it is a mild drink,

almost like juice. In fact, wine coolers are decep-
tive because they can make a drinker just as drunk
as any other kind of alcoholic drink.

A young teen refuses a
drink from her friend.
Kids who are aware of the
damage that alcohol can
cause do not give in to
peer pressure.

Kids are also usually not aware of the long-term
effects of beginning to drink alcohol at a young age.
The consequences of drinking dramatically affect
young people, especially because their bodies are
changing as they go from childhood through adoles-
cence to adulthood. The assault of alcohol is especially
severe on brain cells, where it affects the ability to
learn, and on the reproductive system, where it can
cause irreversible damage. Drinking affects growth
and development in many serious ways, and the
earlier it begins, the more serious the results.

Alcohol and Suicide

Alcohol is a depressant. Although it makes the drinker feel good at first, it later causes an increase in depressed feelings. Because of this reaction, alcohol is a particularly dangerous drug when used by anyone who may be contemplating suicide.

Researchers have shown that 60 percent of all teen suicides are alcohol related, which means that the young person who took his or her own life had used alcohol at some point. Depression often precedes suicide, and alcohol aggravates depression. Not all alcoholics are likely to commit suicide, but for those who have attempted suicide, alcohol is often a contributing factor in later attempts.

There are a number of warning signs to be aware of that are associated with potential suicide:

- a loss of interest in day-to-day activities;
- a withdrawal from family and friends;
- a loss of interest in schoolwork;
- sudden and unexpected changes in behavior; and
- an increase in drinking alcohol.

At the very least, a young person who suffers from these symptoms is depressed. If that person then uses alcohol, his or her condition can only worsen, and the chance of going through with committing suicide is increased.

Drinking can even affect unborn babies. An infant born by a mother who has been drinking during pregnancy may suffer from a series of birth defects called fetal alcohol syndrome (FAS). Babies who suffer from FAS are usually small and underweight at birth. Their central nervous systems are so disrupted by their mothers' drinking that they have learning, memory, and attention disorders. Many are born mentally retarded. As they grow up, they frequently have discipline problems and are poorly coordinated.

Some 40,000 babies a year are born in the United States with FAS. Doctors now recommend that pregnant women avoid all alcohol.

Drinking and Driving

Every year almost 50,000 Americans die in automobile accidents. Of these deaths, about 25,000 are related to alcohol. Consider this number of annual deaths when compared to the Vietnam War, in which nearly 60,000 Americans died—*over an eight-year period*. Or the Persian Gulf War, in which about 300 Americans died.

The legal drinking age in all fifty states is twenty-one. Yet, young people are allowed to apply for a driver's license at age sixteen. Since kids are drinking at increasingly younger ages, some drunk drivers on the roads are under the legal drinking age. In 1991, more than 1.1 million people were arrested for driving while intoxicated (DWI). About 10 percent were under the age of eighteen. All states consider a driver as legally drunk if he or she has more than 0.10 percent blood alcohol concentration in the blood. But even smaller amounts can affect a person's judgment and coordination and slow his or her reflexes when behind the wheel of a car.

In the 1970s, many states lowered the drinking age from twenty-one to eighteen. This followed the lowering of the voting age to eighteen. Many people felt that if people were old enough to vote and to serve in the armed forces, they should also be allowed to drink legally. Unfortunately, over the next few years, the number of drunk-driving accidents and deaths among young people under age twenty-one also rose dramatically. In the 1980s, the federal government stepped in and demanded that the states return the drinking age to twenty-one. By 1988, all the states had done so, and drunk-driving arrests and accidents among young people began to decline.

Drinking and driving are a deadly combination. A drunk driver is a danger to himself or herself, to any passengers, and to other people on the road. Yet, young people continue to drink and drive.

A billboard reminds students of the drastic consequences of drinking and driving. Groups like Students Against Driving Drunk (SADD) encourage other teens to spread the word in their communities.

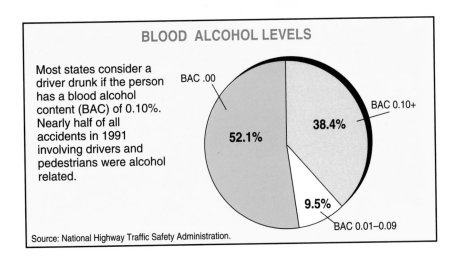

BLOOD ALCOHOL LEVELS

Most states consider a driver drunk if the person has a blood alcohol content (BAC) of 0.10%. Nearly half of all accidents in 1991 involving drivers and pedestrians were alcohol related.

BAC .00

BAC 0.10+

38.4%

52.1%

9.5%

BAC 0.01–0.09

Source: National Highway Traffic Safety Administration.

The Fight Against Drinking and Driving

The legal punishments for drinking and driving are similar from state to state. Those convicted face a suspension or loss of their licenses, fines, and even imprisonment. In thirty-five states, victims are allowed to sue the person who sold the alcohol to the driver if the driver is a minor. Legal punishments, however, have not had a long-term effect on the total number of people who drink and drive.

As a result, many states have adopted other programs along with their legal remedies. In most states, a driver found guilty of driving while intoxicated can choose—or may be required—to take part in an alcohol education or rehabilitation program. Driver education programs in schools also stress the effects of drinking and driving. In addition, groups like Students Against Driving Drunk (SADD) and

Antidrunk-driving devices can be installed in cars to prevent a driver from driving while intoxicated. This device will not allow the car to start if the driver who breathes into it has had too much to drink.

Mothers Against Drunk Driving (MADD) try to publicize the deadly effects of drinking and driving.

Even though drinking under the age of twenty-one is technically illegal, the laws are very difficult to enforce. Alcohol education programs try to teach that if a young person drinks, he or she should act responsibly. For example, if young people are driving to a party where drinking is likely to occur, one of the group should be selected as the designated driver. That person agrees in advance not to drink and accepts the responsibility of driving the rest of the group home after the party. Of course, this applies to adults, too.

Students Against Driving Drunk (SADD)

In 1984, an organization called Students Against Driving Drunk (SADD) was formed. Its purpose is to encourage students not to drink and drive at the same time. Although it does not approve of the drinking of alcohol by people under the legal drinking age, SADD recognizes that some young people will drink anyway—and that they should not drive at the same time, under any circumstances.

SADD chapters have been formed in many schools around the country. The organization publishes a "Contract for Life" (below), and SADD encourages both its members and their parents to sign. Under this agreement, students agree not to drink and drive, and parents agree to help any student who has taken a drink to get home safely, with no questions asked.

CONTRACT FOR LIFE
A Contract for Life Between Parent and Teenager
The SADD Drinking-Driver Contract

Teenager:
I agree to call you for advice and/or transportation at any hour, from any place, if I am ever in a situation where I have been drinking or a friend or date who is driving me has been drinking.

_____
Signature

Parent:
I agree to come and get you at any hour, any place, no questions asked and no argument at that time, or I will pay for a taxi to bring you home safely. I expect we would discuss this issue at a later time.

I agree to seek safe, sober transportation home if I am ever in a situation where I have had too much to drink or a friend who is driving me has had too much to drink.

_____
Signature

_____
Date

S.A.D.D. does not condone drinking by those below the legal drinking age. S.A.D.D. encourages all young people to obey the laws of their state, including laws relating to the legal drinking age.

Distributed by S.A.D.D., "Students Against Driving Drunk"

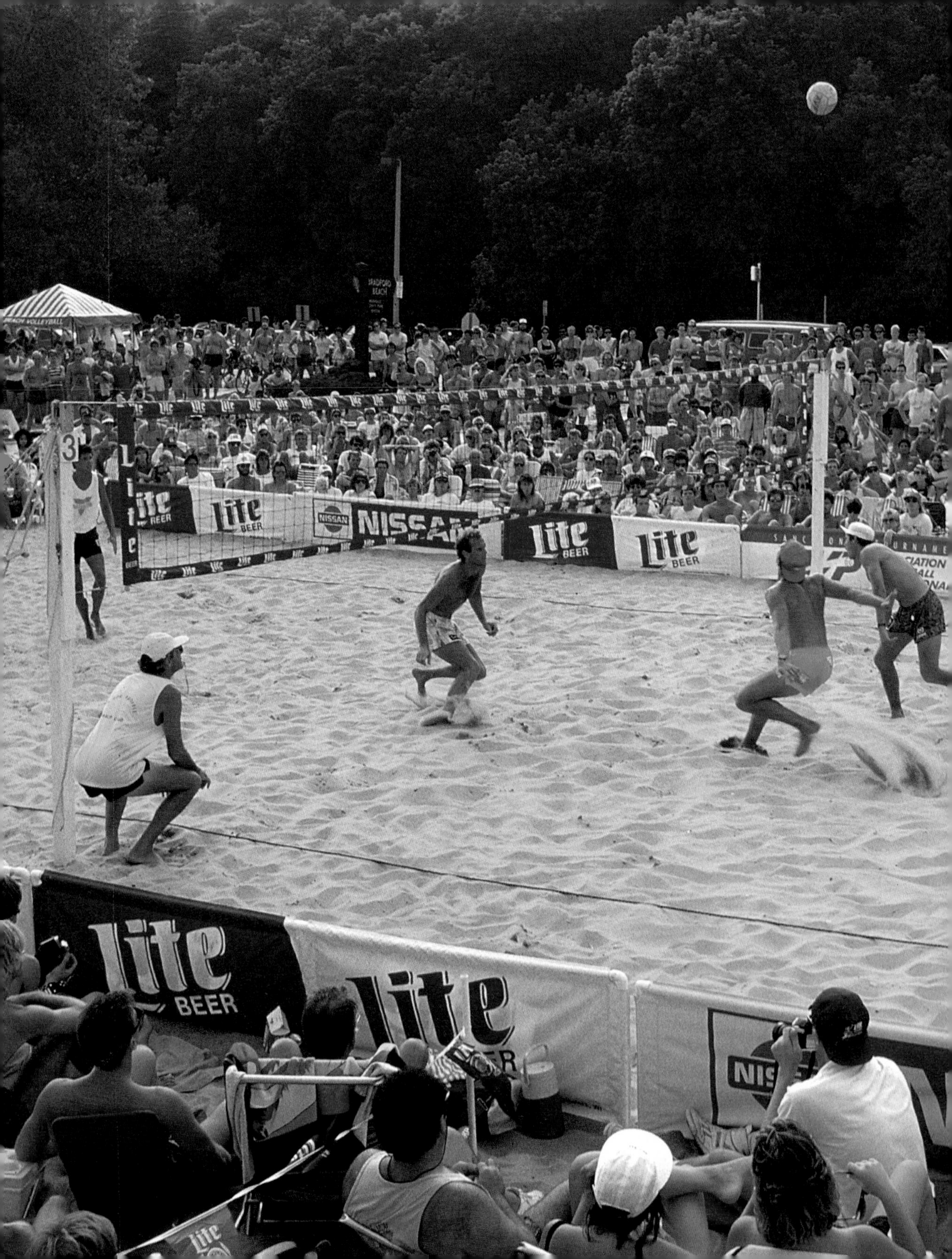

3
Lite BEER
NISSAN
Lite BEER
Lite BEER
Lite BEER

4

Alcohol and the Media

In 1971, cigarette advertisements were banned from television and radio, although ads still may appear in magazines and on billboards. The next year, cigarette advertisements were required to carry a warning label that lists some of the harmful consequences of smoking. Those warnings have appeared on cigarette packs since 1965. Why was such advertising partially banned? The reason was our increasing understanding of the health risks of smoking.

The Glamour of Alcohol Alcohol advertisements share something in common with cigarette advertisements: They both stress the "good times" associated with using their product. The ads

Onlookers at a volleyball game cannot miss seeing the ads for beer. Advertisements for alcohol often emphasize the great times that drinkers have.

suggest that it is glamourous to drink. Young, attractive people are often seen at a party or a picnic having a good time while drinking a beer or a glass of wine. What you will not see is an unattractive person who vomited and passed out on the floor or someone who has died behind the wheel of a wrecked car because of alcohol consumption.

We have learned much about the harmful effects of alcohol abuse. Why has there been less regulation of alcohol advertising? And why are there few warning labels on alcoholic beverages? There are no simple answers to these questions. Alcohol ads appear in a wide variety of publications, and wine and beer ads do appear on television. Ads for hard liquor, however, have been banned from television since the 1980s.

Alcohol advertising is probably not regulated as much as cigarette advertising because alcohol is still not considered dangerous by many people. Our society truly does associate drinking with good times and fun. Thanks to the efforts of antismoking groups, cigarettes are associated with lung cancer and heart disease. Most nonsmokers do not like to inhale the smoke from a smoker's cigarette. But many nondrinkers will tolerate someone who gets tipsy, and may even find it funny.

The glamour and humor of alcohol have a long history in the American media. In the 1930s, for

A massive billboard towers over the field at a professional baseball game. Unlike cigarette ads, alcohol ads are unregulated.

example, the movies of the great comic W. C. Fields were really one long joke about Fields's alcohol abuse. In films such as *My Little Chickadee* and *The Bank Dick*, Fields portrayed a lovable and harassed man whose only escape from a nagging wife or obnoxious children was in the bottle. Fields looked like our image of what a drunk is—he had a red clown's nose and was overweight and sloppy. In real life, Fields did in fact have a severe drinking problem.

Other movies of the time glamourized drinking. *The Thin Man* movies of the 1930s and 1940s were about a glamourous and well-to-do couple named Nick and Nora Charles. Nick was a private eye and Nora was his wise-cracking wife. In all their movies they constantly smoked and drank martinis—and were hung over at one time or another. When this

Nick and Nora Charles were often hung over in *The Thin Man* movies. Here, their dog also appears to have had too much to drink.

movie couple had too much to drink they made funny remarks about it. The overriding message of these movies was that glamourous people like Nick and Nora drink and excessive drinking is something to laugh about.

Although there have always been movies that portrayed the bad effects of drinking—such as *The Lost Weekend* and *Days of Wine and Roses*—the overall picture that was presented in the movie industry tended to associate drinking with glamour and humor.

Early TV also created a stylish or funny association with drinking—even a family program like the popular *I Love Lucy* in the 1950s, starring Lucille Ball and Desi Arnaz as Lucy and Ricky Ricardo, found humor in alcohol. In one episode, Lucy tries to do a TV commercial about a vitamin supplement that, unknown to her, is loaded with alcohol. During the rehearsals, Lucy samples the supplement and gets extremely drunk. By the time she goes on the air, she can barely speak or stand up. Her momentary abuse of alcohol is seen as screamingly funny.

Like the movies of today, TV now takes alcohol abuse a bit more seriously. *Cheers*, a show that ran for eleven seasons until 1993, took place in a bar run by Sam Malone, a recovering alcoholic. The producers developed Sam's character to reinforce their ideas about the seriousness of alcoholism.

The characters portrayed by the cast of *Cheers* had lives that revolved around a neighborhood bar, but the writers took great care to be sure that alcohol abuse was not a source of humor.

"We were worried about the negative aspects of bars," Glen Charles explained in an interview. "We wanted to stay away from drunken humor." Another example is *The John Larroquette Show*, which revolves around a character who is a recovering alcoholic. Even though the show is a situation comedy, the writers have maintained a more serious coverage of alcohol abuse and do not use the disease as the source of humor.

The media does carry fewer alcohol ads than in the past, and the movies and TV tend to take alcohol abuse more seriously, but society's attitudes about alcohol are still more tolerant than they are about other drugs or cigarettes. Research has not proven that there is a connection between positive images of alcohol in the media and an increase in drinking. Advertising and the content of films and TV may be more a reflection of our attitudes as a society toward drinking rather than something that *causes* drinking.

Are Antidrinking Advertising Campaigns Effective? Antidrinking campaigns are often not even aimed at drinking. Instead, they try to educate the drinker about the *consequences* of his or her behavior. For example, Mothers Against Drunk Driving (MADD), which was founded by a group of mothers whose children were killed by drunk drivers, does not try to get people to stop drinking—only to not drink and drive at the same time.

Our country does not have a successful record of antidrinking campaigns. The most famous effort to save people from alcohol was the Eighteenth Amendment to the U.S. Constitution. Called the

Prohibition Amendment, it was in effect from 1920 to 1933. During that time, the manufacture and sale of alcoholic beverages was forbidden throughout the United States. However, people still drank as much as they had before 1920. In the place of the legal manufacture of alcohol came gangster-run bootleg operations that moved in and took over the business. Alcohol was sold in speakeasies—illegal,

In 1990, members of a Harlem church spent a day whitewashing alcohol and cigarette billboards in their community. Antidrinking campaigns have not been very successful in getting people to stop abusing alcohol.

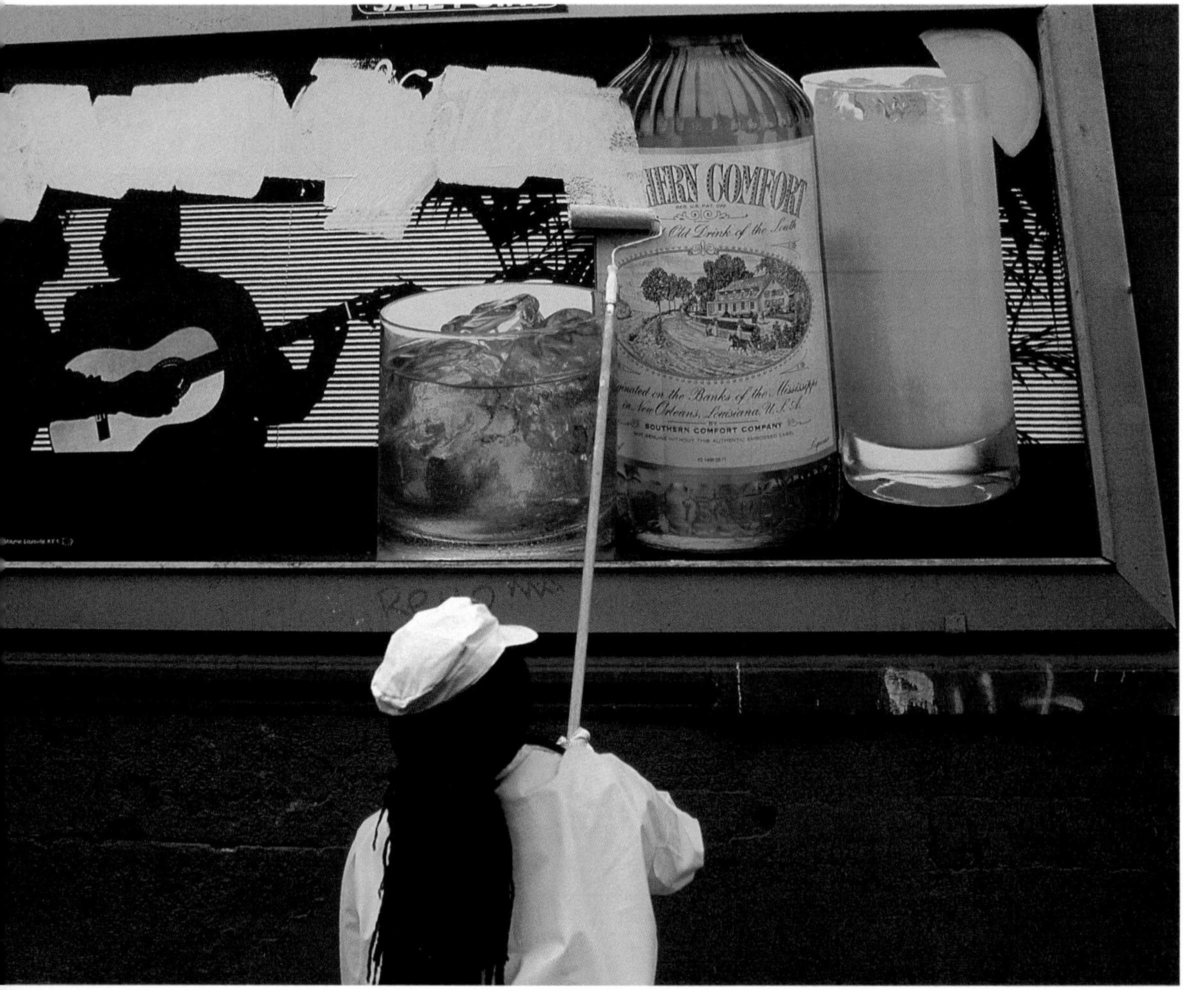
Old Drink of the South
SOUTHERN COMFORT COMPANY

Drugs and the Media

Alcohol is not the only drug portrayed in the media. Marijuana is often seen in movies, and even on TV. An episode of the show *Roseanne* focused on the hilarity of the effects of marijuana when all three adult characters, Roseanne, Dan, and Jackie, shared a marijuana cigarette. This episode also covered some negative aspects of getting high.

Movies such as *The Big Chill* have also shown people having fun together while smoking marijuana and drinking. These images in the media send the message to kids that is okay to use drugs and that ordinary people, who are not considered drug abusers, sometimes use drugs. Many people have wondered if a liberal attitude toward alcohol can lead to drug abuse. The current casual attitude toward drugs and alcohol in the media could prompt further examination of that question.

Researchers, however, have not established a cause-and-effect link between drug use and alcoholism. Apparently, people who are likely to use drugs are just as likely to abuse alcohol, since what they are looking for is to get high. In addition, drug use has become so widespread in our culture that the numbers of people who use both drugs and alcohol have increased over the last twenty years. Some people attribute part of this growth to the portrayal of drugs and alcohol in the media.

secret bars and nightclubs that were found in every city across the country. And some people even made their own alcohol (called bathtub gin), using stills in their homes. Despite the law of the land, people wanted to drink—and they did.

By the 1930s, most politicians realized that Prohibition had failed and that the government could not regulate people's morals. The manufacture and sale of alcohol became legal again in 1933.

With this history, anti-alcohol campaigns have never been successful on a national level. The focus is now on the need to control the negative side effects of alcohol abuse and educate people about the health consequences of drinking too much.

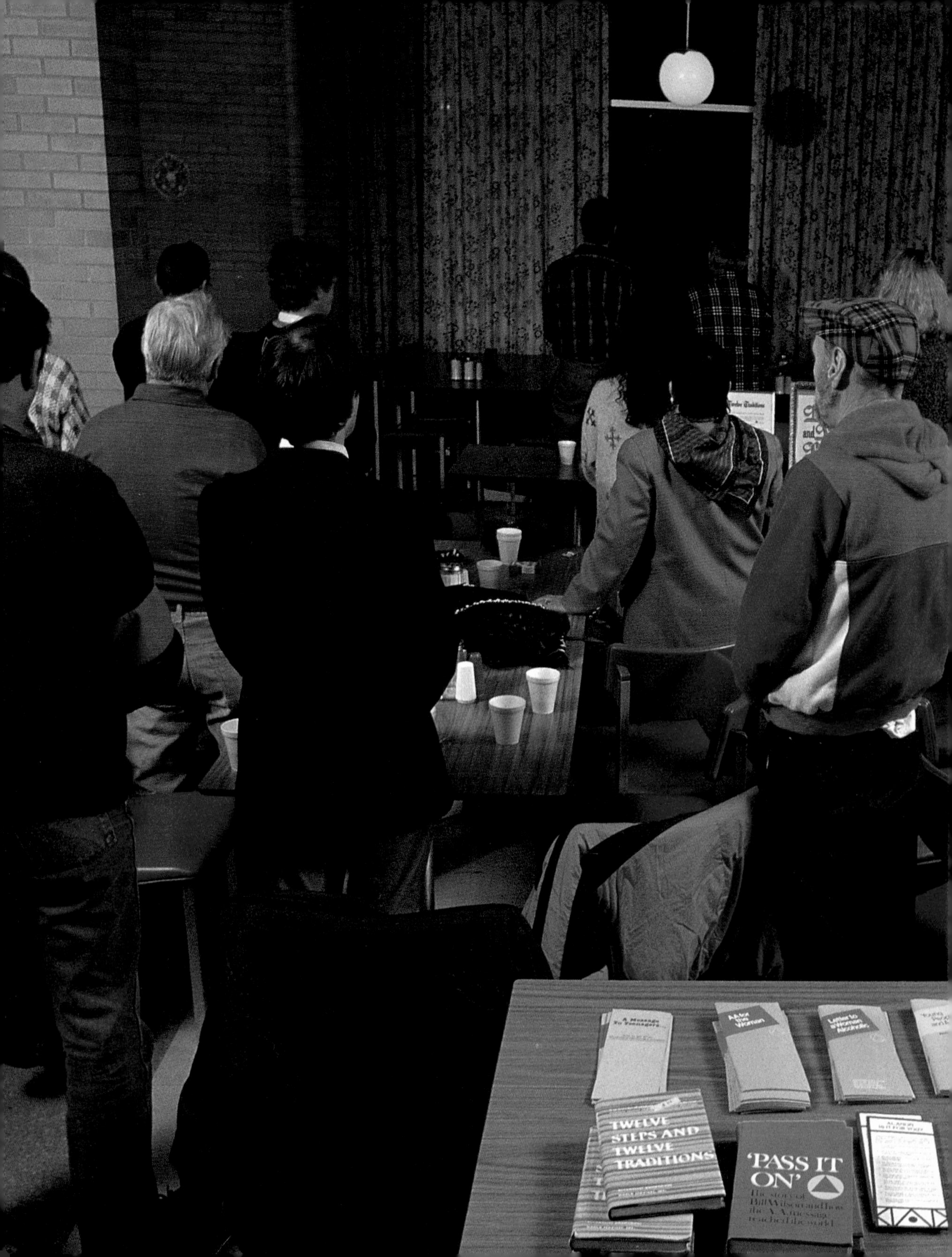

TWELVE STEPS AND TWELVE TRADITIONS
'PASS IT ON'

5

......

Can Alcoholism Be Treated and Cured?

Alcoholism is a progressive disease. That means that the alcoholic's condition grows worse if he or she continues to drink. Although alcoholism cannot be cured, it can be treated. All treatment is based on one major requirement—the alcoholic cannot drink alcohol.

Alcoholics Anonymous

One of the most successful programs to help problem drinkers is called Alcoholics Anonymous (AA). AA is made up of thousands of support groups around the world. Members meet to share their stories

Members of Alcoholics Anonymous (AA) choose not to drink. At AA meetings members can talk about their addiction and get support from people who know what it is like to need alcohol.

about drinking and how it affected their lives. By revealing their alcoholism to others suffering from the disease, alcoholics learn that they are not alone and gain strength through the support of the group.

Alcoholics Anonymous was founded in 1935 by a New York stockbroker and an Ohio physician, both of whom had struggled for years with their alcoholism. They discovered that one of the best medicines for an alcoholic was talking to another alcoholic. Over the years, the AA program of recovery gradually came into being.

AA is based on the Twelve-Step program and the belief that an AA member who follows these steps will begin to recover from alcoholism. The Twelve Steps start by asking the alcoholic to acknowledge his or her powerlessness over alcohol.

Taking it day by day, the alcoholic chooses not to drink. Attending AA meetings on a regular basis, daily for the first three months, keeps the alcoholic in contact with others in AA and with the principles of the program. In addition to not drinking, members of AA seek a life that is less self-centered and devote themselves to helping others who wish to recover from their disease.

When AA was founded, alcoholism was still looked on as a human and moral weakness. Because of the shame attached to alcoholism, early AA members did not reveal their complete identities to

The Twelve Steps of Alcoholics Anonymous

The Twelve Steps at first appears to be quite religious. It isn't; it's spiritual. All references to God are symbolic. The steps revolve around an image called a higher power: some imaginary being that is stronger than the person and is able to guide him or her through life's tough spots. The steps are as follows:

1. We admitted we were powerless over alcohol—that our lives had become unmanageable.
2. Came to believe that a Power greater than ourselves could restore us to sanity.
3. Made a decision to turn our will and our lives over to the care of God *as we understood Him*.
4. Made a searching and fearless moral inventory of ourselves.
5. Admitted to God, to ourselves, and to another human being the exact nature of our wrongs.
6. Were entirely ready to have God remove all these defects of character.
7. Humbly asked Him to remove our shortcomings.
8. Made a list of all persons we had harmed and became willing to make amends to them.
9. Made direct amends to such people wherever possible, except when to do so would injure them or others.
10. Continued to take personal inventory, and when we were wrong, promptly admitted it.
11. Sought through prayer and meditation to improve our conscious contact with God *as we understood Him*, praying only for knowledge of His will for us and the power to carry that out.
12. Having had a spiritual awakening as a result of these Steps, we tried to carry this message to alcoholics and to practice these principles in all our affairs.

the group. For example, if your name was Mary Jones, you would introduce yourself in your AA group as "Mary." By remaining anonymous, an AA member does not have to fear being exposed to less-understanding people in the community.

Over the years, anonymity has remained a major foundation of AA. Members who practice the Twelve Steps believe that remaining anonymous is an important part of recovery in AA. They feel it helps stress the importance of principles and the group over the ego of the individual.

Most countries of the world today have Alcoholics Anonymous groups. The AA program has shown that it can be successful in many different cultures. As a result, millions of people have begun their recovery in AA and are now living productive and fulfilling lives.

Other Treatment Programs

In the sixty years since the founding of AA, several new forms of treatment have emerged. As our understanding of alcoholism as a real disease has grown, many of these new forms of treatment have come to us from the worlds of medicine and science.

Detoxification and Rehabilitation

When AA was founded, people suffering from advanced stages of alcoholism were usually sent to mental institutions. Doctors had little or no under-standing of how to treat the alcohol abuser. Today, however, a number of medical treatments are avail-able. For example, people suffering from severe alcoholism may be admitted to detoxification cen-ters in hospitals, where they can be treated with medications that help them through the difficult early periods of withdrawal from alcohol.

People who have been drinking severely over long periods of time may suffer from delirium tremens (DTs) when they withdraw suddenly from alcohol.

The DTs are a frightening experience. The alcoholic has visual and sometimes audio hallucinations and shakes uncontrollably from head to foot. He or she may also be violently ill, and the symptoms may last for days or weeks.

Rehabilitation centers, like this one in Pennsylvania, are available to help many people cope with alcohol and other drug addictions.

SUBSTANCE ABUSE TREATMENT

		All Clients	Alcoholism Clients Only	Percentage of Alcohol Patients
TOTAL		794,755	290,031	36%
TYPE OF CARE	Detoxification	11,091	4,004	36%
	Rehab/Residential	83,193	16,792	20%
	Ambulatory	700,471	269,235	38%
LOCATION OF TREATMENT	Hospital	82,645	21,788	26%
	Community mental health care	129,913	56,676	44%
	Free-standing nonresidential facility	423,840	173,943	41%
	Correctional facility	24,746	2,447	10%
	Halfway house	16,945	4,939	29%
	Other residential facility	53,670	13,457	25%
	Other site	7,033	2,391	34%
	Multiple sites	32,136	11,880	37%
	Unknown	23,136	2,519	11%

Source: U.S. Substance Abuse and Mental Health Services Administration and the U.S. Institute on Alcohol Abuse and Alcoholism, "Highlights from the National Drug and Alcoholism Treatment Unit Survey: 1992 and Selected Trends."

Once the alcoholic has been detoxed, he or she may be admitted to a rehabilitation center—"rehabs," for short. Rehab programs last a minimum of twenty-eight days and may run longer depending on the severity of the alcoholic's illness. Patients in rehabs attend group therapy sessions, where they talk with other alcoholics and a psychotherapist. They also attend regular AA meetings in the rehab facility and see an individual counselor. The rehab experience is highly structured, with the patient expected to perform his or her chores (such as cleaning one's room) and to show up for group sessions and AA meetings. One of the major objectives of rehabilitation is to help patients overcome their denial of the fact that they cannot control their drinking. This denial is a very deeply rooted part of alcoholism, and it stands in the way of the alcoholic's recovery.

Drug Therapies

Some alcoholics are so ill that they may require strong medications to help them avoid alcohol. One of the most commonly used drugs in the treatment of alcoholism is Antabuse, which is used to treat patients whose compulsion to drink is overwhelming. If a person takes Antabuse and then drinks, he or she becomes ill.

Some doctors have recently begun using a drug called Naltrexone to treat alcoholics. In the past, Naltrexone had been used mainly to treat people addicted to narcotics. Doctors discovered, however, that it could also have a positive effect on some alcoholics. Naltrexone blocks the effects of alcohol and makes the patient physically uncomfortable— thereby breaking the drinking cycle.

Drug therapies are an important part of treating alcoholism. But they are only a small part of recovery. In order to begin recovery and enjoy a full life, an alcoholic must honestly face his or her disease and accept responsibility for getting better.

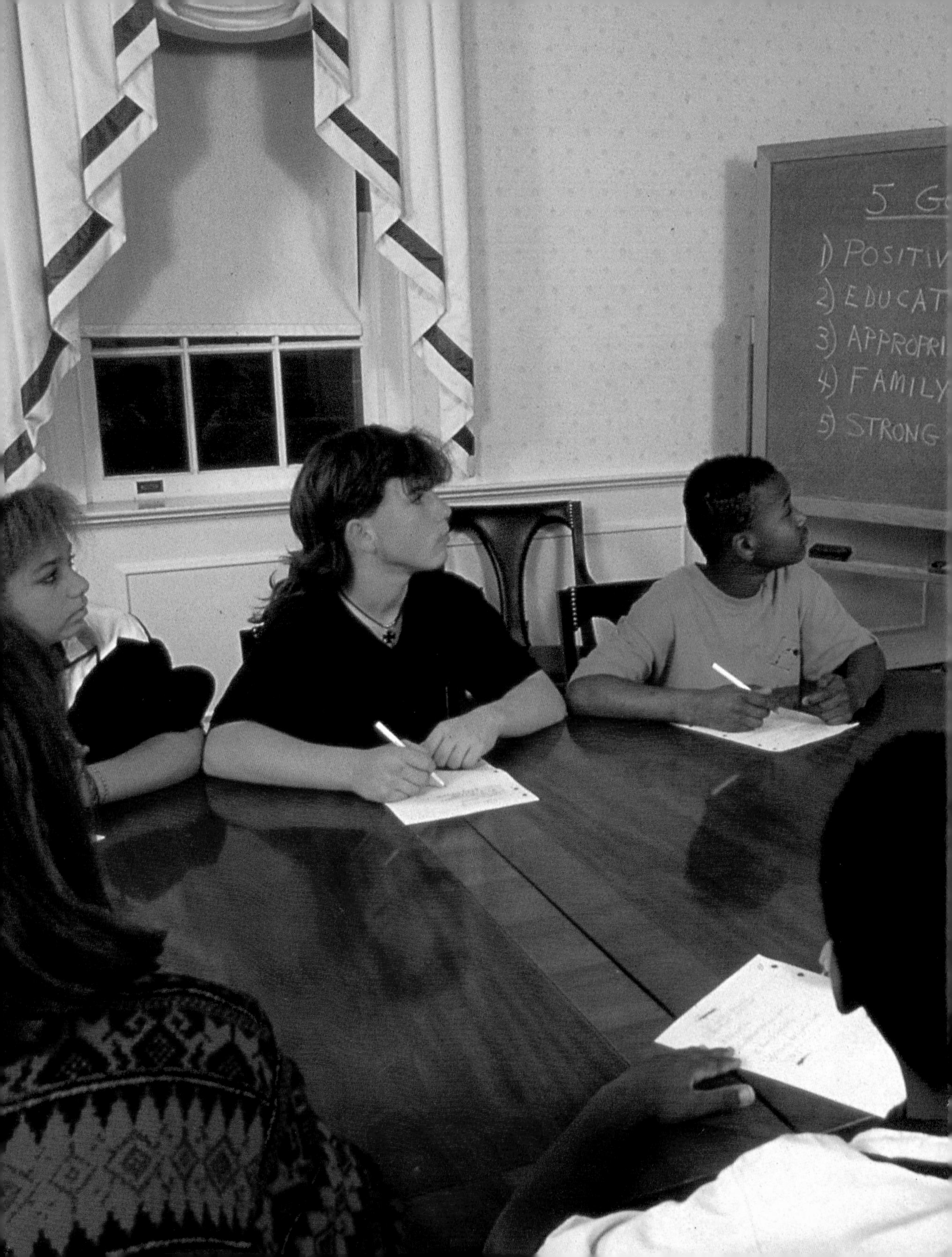
5 G
1) POSITIV
2) EDUCAT
3) APPROPRI
4) FAMILY
5) STRONG

Where Can I Go for Help?

Where can a young person go for help if he or she is coping with alcoholism in the family? The first—and most important thing to remember—is that you are not alone. Millions of people face these same problems. Of course, before looking for help, you must be ready to acknowledge that there is a problem. These first steps are often the hardest to take, since denial and the urge to protect our family and loved ones often prevent us from going outside for assistance. Remember: you have choices.

Al-Anon and Alateen

Al-Anon was started in the 1930s by Lois Wilson, the wife of Bill Wilson, one of the founders of Alcoholics Anonymous.

Counseling and other services are available to young people who are coping with alcoholism in their families.

Even before the term *co-dependence* had been invented, Lois realized that she had her own problems as a wife of an alcoholic—and later, a whole different set of problems as the wife of a recovering alcoholic.

Al-Anon was created for the spouses of active or recovering alcoholics. Its early membership was overwhelmingly female, a reflection of the fact that the majority of early AA members were male. (In the 1930s, alcoholism was seen largely as a male problem.) Today, Al-Anon has both male and female members.

Al-Anon uses the same Twelve Step program as AA. Its members meet in groups, where they share their experiences and receive support from the group. The Twelve Step program also works in this context because the Al-Anon member admits that he or she is also powerless over alcohol (or the alcoholic).

Al-Anon members work at keeping the focus on themselves. In addition to acknowledging that they don't have control over the alcoholic, they come to realize and accept that they did not cause the disease and they cannot cure it. They go to Al-Anon meetings, where they share their experiences, receive group support, and learn the skills necessary to take care of their own needs first. As part of their recovery, Al-Anon members learn to stop trying to

Betty Ford Helps America Understand Alcoholism

Betty Ford, the wife of former president Gerald R. Ford, was First Lady of the United States from 1974 to 1977. During her two-and-a-half years as First Lady, Betty Ford became very popular with the American public. She was known for her honesty and outspokenness on many issues, including the operation for breast cancer that she underwent in 1974.

When President Ford was defeated for re-election, he and his wife retired to a new home in southern California. After an exciting life in the White House, retirement proved difficult for Betty Ford. For many years she had suffered from a pinched nerve in her neck, and in retirement, the condition seemed to worsen. To relieve the constant pain, Mrs. Ford took medications prescribed by her doctor. She had always been a social drinker. In California, Mrs. Ford continued to enjoy alcohol, but she also continued to take her pain medications regularly.

Her family began to notice a difference in her behavior. More and more, Mrs. Ford began to fall asleep in public. She also started to slur her words and appear drowsy and sedated much of the time. Her children and husband consulted experts on cross addiction—having an addiction to alcohol and drugs at the same time. They decided to have an intervention, in which the family would sit down with Mrs. Ford and confront her with what they were observing about her behavior. The objective of the intervention was to help Mrs. Ford face her problem and accept responsibility and treatment for it.

The intervention was very emotional. Mrs. Ford agreed that she had a problem and needed

Betty Ford has been an inspiration to people in need of treatment for alcohol and drug abuse.

to seek help for it. Within a few days, she entered a rehabilitation center and began her recovery from alcoholism and dependency on prescription medications.

True to her open and honest nature, Betty Ford told the public about her experiences and urged others with similar problems to seek help. She hoped that if a former First Lady could admit a problem involving the abuse of alcohol and prescription drugs, then maybe others would not be afraid to step forward and do something about their own addictions.

Today, the hospital in San Diego where Betty Ford was treated is named in her honor. Many thousands of alcoholics have faced up to their problem and sought help at the Betty Ford Center. Mrs. Ford, who is now in her seventies, continues to work with others in recovery. Perhaps because of her courageousness in the face of overwhelming personal crises, she still remains one of the most popular women in America.

control the alcoholic's drinking. And they learn to stop making excuses for the alcoholic as well.

Learning not to be involved in the alcoholic's disease is probably the most difficult lesson of all to understand. Most people in relationships with alcoholics spend years trying to help the alcoholic—usually by trying to control his or her drinking in some way. Al-Anon teaches its members to do the exact opposite: If you really want to help the alcoholic in the long run, you must step back and let him or her face the consequences of drinking—even when those consequences are devastating.

A more recent offshot of Al-Anon is Alateen, which is a version of Al-Anon for young people between the ages of twelve and twenty. Members of Alateen can relate to each other as peers, sharing their feelings about the unique problems of growing up in an alcoholic family. Al-Anon and Alateen meetings are free and open to anyone who wishes to attend. All you need to do is show up. Alatot is also available for children under the age of twelve.

Individual and Family Counseling

In addition to turning to support groups such as Al-Anon, Alateen, and Alatot, many people involved in relationships with alcoholics also seek individual and family counseling. Your school guidance office is one place to go for information, or you could speak with a religious leader. The first step—a willingness to discuss the problem with someone else—is always the most difficult. But once you have done that, you will discover a world of people who are waiting to help.

Individual or family therapy can be expensive. Some counselors and therapists work on a sliding-fee basis, which means that their fee is based on a person's ability to pay. Others provide their services at no charge at all.

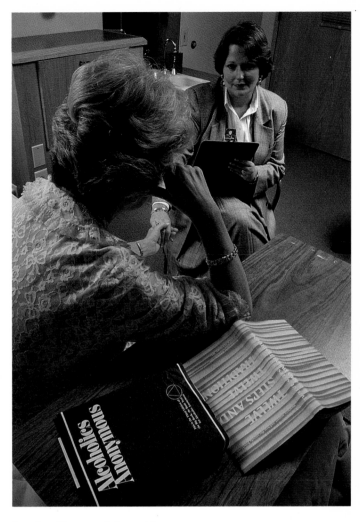

Individuals can receive counseling and support at an alcohol treatment center.

Family therapy treats the alcoholic problem in group meetings of the entire family. At these sessions, the counselor acts as a mediator, encouraging all members of the family—the drinker as well as those affected by his or her drinking—to honestly express their feelings, especially ones of anger and guilt. Healing can begin only after feelings have come out into the open.

Interventions A relatively new technique used to help alcoholics face their drinking problem is intervention. An intervention occurs when family members confront the alcoholic and ask him or her to acknowledge that alcohol has taken control. To be effective, the intervention must be done in an atmosphere of love and concern, but at the same time it must be honest and direct. If it is effective, the alcoholic will be able to break through his or her denial and be willing to get help.

An intervention should never be done without the advice and guidance of a therapist or counselor who is experienced in such work. It may not be the appropriate approach in all situations and could produce disastrous results if used incorrectly.

Where to Write or Call for Information

The following organizations publish literature on alcoholism and are good places to contact when you are looking for information and assistance:

Al-Anon/Alateen Family Groups
P.O. Box 862
Midtown Station
New York, NY 10018-0862
1-800-356-9996

Alcoholics Anonymous
General Service Office
P.O. Box 45
Grand Central Station
New York, NY 10163
212-870-3400

Mothers Against Drunk Driving (MADD)
511 E. John Carpenter Freeway, Suite 700
Irving, TX 75062
1-800-438-6233 or 1-800-GET-MADD

National Clearinghouse for Alcohol and
Drug Information
P.O. Box 2345
Rockville, MD 20847-2345
1-800-729-6686

Students Against Driving Drunk (SADD)
P.O. Box 800
Marlboro, MA 01752
508-481-3568 (Voice Mail)

Glossary

AA Alcoholics Anonymous—the largest self-help group of recovering alcoholics, with programs around the world.

ACOAs Term referring to the adult children of alcoholics—adults who grew up within an alcoholic family.

Al-Anon Self-help group for those who have a relationship with an alcoholic.

Alateen Self-help group for teenagers living in an alcoholic family.

alcoholic A person suffering from the disease of alcoholism.

alcoholism A disease in which a person is unable to stop drinking alcohol even though it causes harm.

COAs Term that refers to the children of alcoholics—children who grew up in an alcoholic family.

co-dependence Term referring to an unhealthy way of living, thinking, and coping that results from living in an alcoholic family.

denial A psychological defense mechanism that allows a person (in this case, the alcoholic) to avoid admitting that he or she has a serious problem (excessive drinking of alcohol).

detoxification Treatment given to people suffering from severe alcoholism that allows them to stabilize.

DTs Delirium Tremens—a severe withdrawal reaction from alcohol characterized by hallucinations and violent shaking.

DWI Driving while intoxicated—a legal offense in all fifty states.

FAS Fetal Alcohol Syndrome—a series of birth defects that affect children of mothers who drank during pregnancy.

intervention An event in which the family of an alcoholic, under the guidance of a professional, confronts the alcoholic and asks him or her to be honest about drinking.

MADD Mothers Against Drunk Driving—a group of mothers whose children were killed by drunk drivers. They are dedicated to convincing people not to drive when they have been drinking.

Naltrexone A drug used to treat people in withdrawal from narcotics; now used for the treatment of alcohol as well.

rehabilitation Treatment programs for recovering alcoholics that combine a structured environment, group therapy, and AA meetings. Patients attend for a minimum of twenty-eight days.

SADD Students Against Driving Drunk—organized by students to encourage their peers not to drink and drive at the same time. Developed the Contract for Life.

For Further Reading

Berger, Gilda. *Alcoholism and the Family*. New York: Franklin Watts, 1993.

Diamond, Arthur. *Alcoholism*. San Diego, CA: Lucent Books, 1992.

Harris, Jaqueline L. *Drugs and Disease*. New York: Twenty-First Century Books, 1993.

Hyde, Margaret O. *Alcohol: Uses and Abuses*. New Jersey: Enslow, 1988.

Nielsen, Nancy. *Teen Alcoholism*. San Diego, CA: Lucent Books, 1990.

Rosenberg, Maxine. *Not My Family: Sharing the Truth about Alcoholism*. New York: Macmillan, 1988.

Salak, John. *Drugs in Society: Are They Our Suicide Pill?* New York: Twenty-First Century Books, 1993.

Source Notes

Alcoholics Anonymous, 3rd ed. New York: Alcoholics Anonymous World Services, Inc. 1976.

Claypool, Jane. *Alcohol and Teens*. New York: Messner, 1985.

Cohen, Susan, and Daniel Cohen. *A Six-Pack and a Fake I.D.: Teens Look at the Drinking Question*. New York: M. Evans and Company, 1986.

Goleman, Daniel. "Family Rituals May Promote Better Adjustment." *New York Times*, March 11, 1992.

Goodnough, Abby. "Recovering from Divorce and Alcohol." *New York Times*, December 8, 1994.

Greenberg, Keith. *Charles, Burrows, & Charles: TV's Top Producers*. Woodbridge, CT: Blackbirch Press, 1995.

Living Sober New York: Alcoholics Anonymous World Services, Inc., 1975.

National Council on Alcoholism and Drug Dependence, *Youth and Alcohol: A National Survey*. Washington, D.C., June 14, 1991.

National Institute on Alcohol Abuse and Alcoholism, *Fetal Alcohol Syndrome*. July 1991.

National Institute on Drug Abuse/University of Michigan Institute for Social Research, *Drug Use: America's Students*, 1994.

Sheehan, Martha. "Survey Reveals High Rate of Exposure to Alcoholism." *Recovery Press*, December, 1991.

U.S. Department of Health and Human Services, Office of Substance Abuse Prevention, *What's Important About Children of Alcoholics*.

Index

Photo Credits

Cover and pages 4, 12 : ©Superstock; p. 6: ©James Pozarik/Gamma Liaison; p. 8: ©A. Glauberman/Photo Researchers, Inc.; p. 18: ©Will & Deni McIntyre/Photo Researchers, Inc.; pp. 20, 27: ©Richard Hutchings/Photo Researchers, Inc.; p. 22: ©Jeff Greenberg/ Photo Researchers, Inc.; p. 25: ©Barbara Rios/Photo Researchers, Inc.; p. 30: ©Cynthia Dopkin/Photo Researchers, Inc.; p. 32: ©Gamma Liaison; p. 34: ©James Schnepf/ Gamma Liaison; p. 37: ©S. Silverman/Gamma Liaison; p. 38: Culver Pictures, Inc.; p. 40: CHEERS ©1995 by Paramount Pictures; p. 42: ©Stephen Ferry/Gamma Liaison; p. 44: ©Hank Morgan/Science Source/Photo Researchers, Inc.; p. 49: ©Blair Seitz/Photo Researchers, Inc.; p. 52: ©Bachmann/Photo Researchers, Inc.; p.p. 55: ©Bob Riha/ Gamma Liaison; p. 57: ©Spencer Grant/Photo Researchers, Inc.
Charts and graphs by Blackbirch Graphics, Inc.

Acknowledgments

The Twelve Steps are reprinted with permission of Alcoholics Anonymous World Services, Inc. Permission to reprint the Twelve Steps does not mean that A.A. is in any way affiliated with this program. A.A. is a program of recovery from alcoholism only— use of the Twelve Steps in connection with programs and activities which are patterned after A.A., but which address other problems, does not imply otherwise.